# Who Wants to Travel the Great Wall with Me?

## 谁来陪我走长城

**Illustrator:** Yang Zi
**Managing Editor:** Lan Peijin
**Translator:** Zhang Shaoning
**English Editor:** Paul White, Yu Ling
**Designer:** Yuan Qing et al.

First Edition 2005

# Who Wants to Travel the Great Wall with Me?

ISBN 7-119-04180-0

© Foreign Languages Press

Published by Foreign Languages Press
24 Baiwanzhuang Road, Beijing 100037, China
Home Page: http://www.flp.com.cn
E-mail Addresses: info@flp.com.cn
                  sales@flp.com.cn

Distributed by China International Book Trading Corporation
35 Chegongzhuang Xilu, Beijing, 100044, China
P.O. Box 399, Beijing, China
*Printed in the People's Republic of China*

# Who Wants to Travel the Great Wall with Me?

谁来陪我走长城

**Foreign Languages Press**

外 文 出 版 社

# Walking Along the Great Wall

The hunter built a wall
To fend off wolves.
It only kept the sheep in; it failed to keep off the wolves.
But the Great Wall still stretches afar,
Enduring wind and weather.

This childhood rhyme has remained clear in my memory, each word like a heavy brick from the wall, lying in the loneliest corner of my heart. It is hard to remove them, so they have been there for decades.

The shape of the Great Wall closely resembles the Chinese "dragon" totem–endlessly long, curving, lying along high mountains, now appearing now hiding....

The Great Wall we talk about today refers to the one in northern China, the construction of which started in the Qin Dynasty (221-206 BC). It runs for over 5,000 km, from Lintao in Gansu Province in the west to eastern Liaoning Province in the east. It also refers to the over-10,000-km Han Dynasty (206 BC-220 AD) Great Wall, which extends westward along the Silk Road, passing Jiuquan, Dunhuang and Lop Nur. The Great Wall also includes the part built in the Ming Dynasty some six centuries ago. The Great Wall has been regarded as a part of the world's cultural heritage for its long history and its gigantic length.

What would you think of when walking along the Great Wall? If it had been fortified strongly enough to keep out the nomadic tribes, today's China would be very different and much smaller. But the nomadic tribes broke through the Great Wall many times, and some even became rulers of the territory south of it, making the Chinese nation a big family of many ethnic groups, and turning the Great Wall into a beautiful vista within China's territory. Looking back at history, we can see from the Great Wall both the greatness of the defenders and the valiance of the attackers. Today, wars along the Great Wall seem like duels between rivals in love triangles or strife between brothers, and the Great Wall has been and will always be a pride of the Chinese nation.

The Great Wall is like a husband with two wives – the farming people and the nomadic people. It is also like violin strings on which spirited music and soft music are played in turn, staging glory and dreams, prosperity and decline, unity and separation, life and death, love and hatred....

The Great Wall is an extreme of magnificence, almost incomparable with any other manmade landscape. What do you see walking on the Great Wall? It winds its way across countless mountains and ridges, vast grasslands and deserts, joining hundreds of passes and thousands of watchtowers and beacon towers. One can imagine smoke rising from the beacon towers where signal fires were lit in the past.

Walking along the Great Wall, I have seen sunrise at Jiayu Pass, sunset at Shanhai Pass, the sea of clouds below the Wangjing Tower, snow-covered Jinshanling, green pine trees and cypresses at Juyong Pass, red leaves at the Mutianyu section, precipitous peaks at Badaling, the vast sea at Laolongtou.... Meng Jiangnü's lamentations seem to be drifting in the wind. Is it for her husband who died of exhaustion in the construction of the Great Wall, or for the damage done to the wall by weathering and human activities? The gigantic body of the Great Wall is aging and withering little by little. Will it become a mere legend in a hundred years' time?

I dearly love and ache for the Great Wall extending westward, and the barren, desolate lands it passes through. So I cannot be a light-hearted tourist. My heart beats with every curve of the Great Wall. I shall seek it, go close to it, worship it, commemorate it, protect it.

Let us walk along the Great Wall.

The part of the wall built by the State of Chu in the 7th or 8th centuries BC is the earliest Great Wall known so far. In 221 BC, Emperor Qin Shihuang, pictured here, conquered the other six states into which China had been divided, and joined the walls of the states of Qin, Zhao and Yan to form the "Great Wall of Ten Thousand *Li*," reaching as far as Lintao in Gansu Province in the west and eastern Liaoning Province in the east.

◁ Defensive trenches appeared before recorded history. Were they made to ward off enemies or floods? In any case, they were embryonic forms of the Great Wall.

The location of the Han Dynasty Yumen Pass is still a matter of dispute. But "A Tartar under the willows plays a lament on his flute. The spring breeze never blows to him through the Jade Pass" is a verse well known for centuries.

◁ We are all familiar with the story "Baiting the Dukes with False Signal Fires." Would similar things happen today?

The Ming Dynasty (1368-1644) Great Wall extends more than 6,500 km, from the bank of the Yalu River in northeast China to Jiayu Pass in northwest China, passing the Yanshan, Taihang and Helan mountain ranges, and the Gobi Desert. It counts for only one tenth of the total length of the wall built throughout Chinese history.

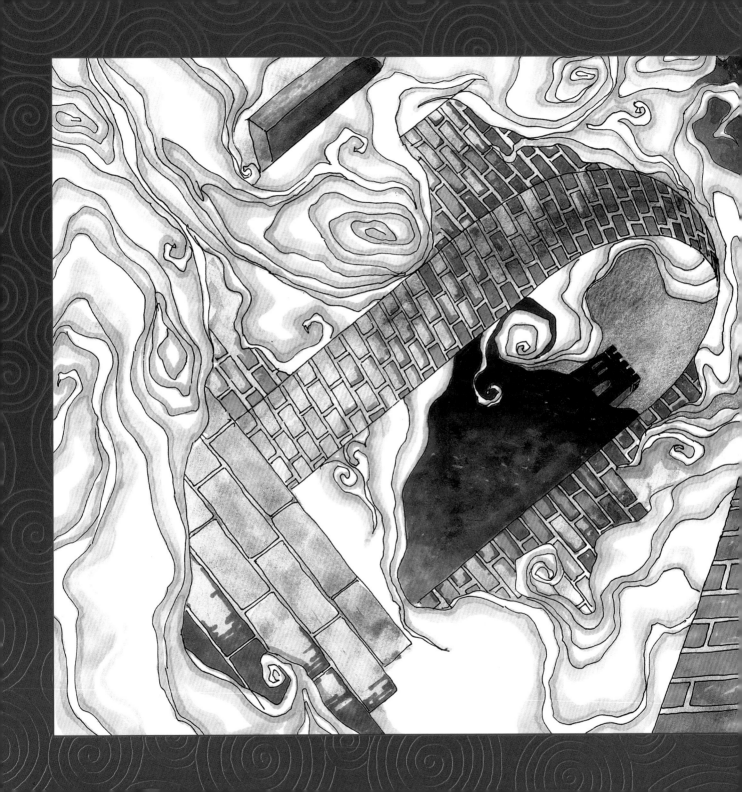

The story of Meng Jiangnü weeping until part of the Great Wall fell has been told for more than a millennium. How can modern people understand this?

No one can count the number of people who died in building the Great Wall, not to mention the cost. In the mid-16th century, the Ming general Qi Jiguang spent 11 million taels of silver (the annual national revenue of the whole country was only four million taels of silver at that time) building or rebuilding the Great Wall from Shanhai Pass to east of Juyong Pass.

◁ A typical watchtower on the Great Wall consists of the base, central room and blockhouse for a lookout post on the top. The base is an elevated section made of rectangular stone slabs, with no windows. The middle part is made of brick, with arched doorways facing north, south, east and west.

Shrouded in snow, the Great Wall looks like it was carved out of jade.

At over 2,000 m above sea level, Wangjing Tower is the highest point on the Beijing section of the Great Wall. It is said that a god turned rocks into goats with his magic whip, drove them up the mountain, and then turned them back into rocks and built the tower with them. Below is a seemingly bottomless abyss.

Who was ever defeated by the cannon known as the "Great Invincible General"? In spite of it, the huge Manchu army broke into the Central Plains. How could this solid Great Wall not fend off the Manchu invaders?

On the Great Wall, I see both the greatness of the defender and the courage of the attacker.

The hunter built a wall to fend off wolves. But it only kept the sheep in; it failed to keep off the wolves.

"Can't you see the piles of human bones under the Great Wall?" How would mankind be with-
out those wars?

The Great Wall is like a mouth with large teeth, ready to devour people.

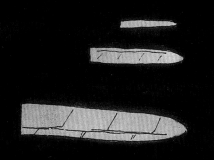

The nomad cavalry broke through the Great Wall, and conquered larger and larger areas. That's why China has such a large territory today. Now, everywhere there is peace.

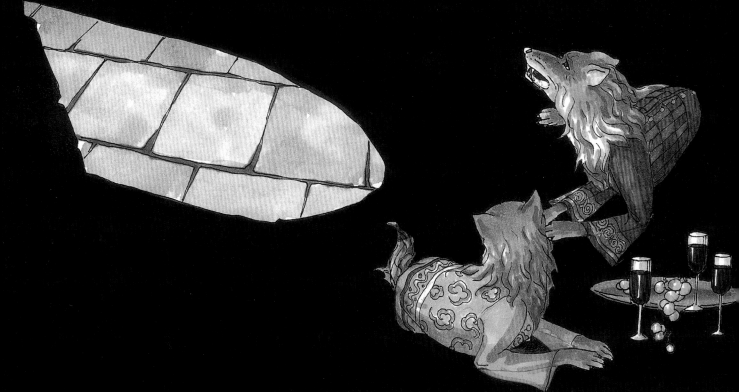

In the Han Dynasty, Zhang Qian and Ban Chao passed here on their way to foreign countries. Merchants from India, Pakistan, Afghanistan, Iran and other South, Central and Western Asian countries entered China from here. The Great Wall was no barrier to exchanges between countries and peoples.

◁ The Great Wall was roughly the dividing line between the nomadic and farming people of north China. I call the people living south of the Great Wall "sheep," and those living north of it "wolves." The Great Wall has witnessed the glory and dreams, prosperity and decline, unification and separation, life and death, and love and hatred of the sheep and the wolves.

The Great Wall records the growth and development of the Chinese nation for over two millennia.

The flanking walls were built for enclosing fields, not for the garrison or for defense.

Is it possible that the Great Wall could turn into a mere "legend" in a hundred years' time?

Juyong Pass,
the western entrance to Beijing,
was a military target for centuries.
It is also renowned for its magnificent scenery.

The eastern end of the Great Wall is called "Old Dragon's Head," because it looks like a dragon's head lowered into the sea.

How many people really understand the desolate, yet splendid, beauty of the Great Wall?

The rich colors of autumn have been a source of inspiration to countless poets. What poetry can I compose on this wall, dappled like a tiger skin? Should I praise the magnificence of the Great Wall or condemn the cruelty of bygone rulers?

In the sunlight, the Great Wall looks majestic, as if it had been made by the hand of God.

The sun, mountains, wind and clouds are loyal friends of the Great Wall, silently witnessing the changes in the human world together with it.

The Great Wall silently winds its way westward, passing through vast deserts. The total length of the Great Wall, winding through 16 provinces, municipalities and autonomous regions, is over 50,000 km.

The curving Great Wall crosses the Yellow River in three places, each forming a majestic landscape.

There were nine garrison areas along the Great Wall: Liaodong, Ji, Xuanfu, Datong, Shanxi, Yulin, Ningxia, Guyuan and Gansu, and their administrative centers were known as the "nine important frontier towns." Now I'm in Yulin.

The Great Wall was not merely a defense work. It was a complete system, combining military and civil ▷
administration. It included barracks, storehouses, roads, bridges, post stations, government offices, state
farms and residential areas. I was a guard at the storehouse on the Jinshanling section of the Great Wall.

A beacon tower dating from the Han Dynasty west of Yumen Pass.

Jiayu Pass in the Gobi Desert, the western end of the Ming Dynasty Great Wall, faces the snow-covered Qilian Mountains to the south and the vast desert to the north. Is the hazy fortress before my eyes the one at Jiayu Pass or a mere mirage?

◁ The Ming Dynasty Great Wall is wide enough for five battle steeds or 10 soldiers to march side by side.

Do you want to see a scene of the construction of the Great Wall? There are many stories about it.

Can you imagine the Great Wall of the State of Qi? The history associated with it has become as hazy as a dream with the passing of time.

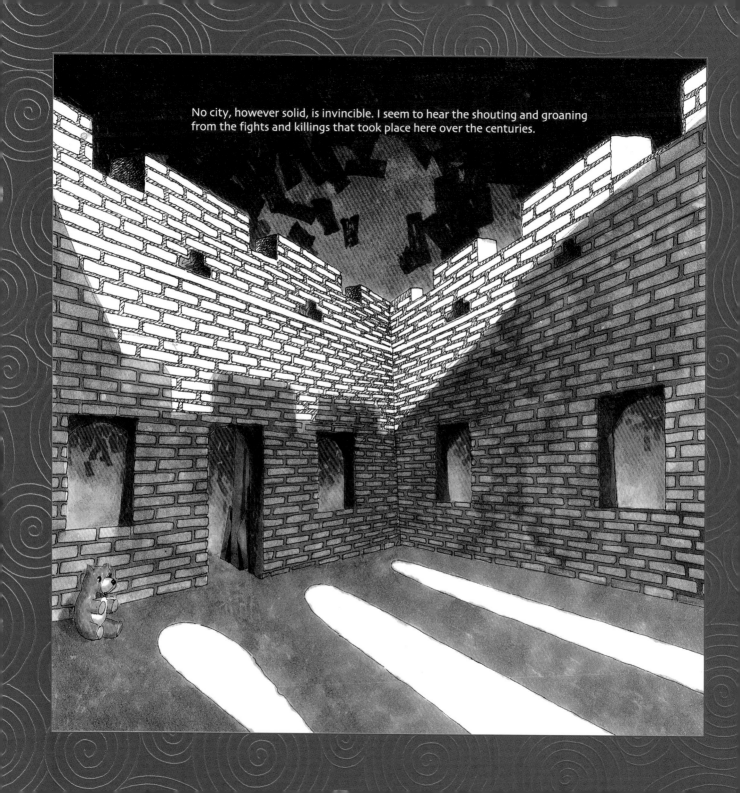

No city, however solid, is invincible. I seem to hear the shouting and groaning from the fights and killings that took place here over the centuries.

Shanhai Pass is linked to the Yanshan Mountain Range to the north, and faces the Bohai Sea to the south. It is a key junction between north China and the three provinces in the northeast. It was traditionally known as "the sole key to the Western Capital, and the First Pass in the Great Wall." Here, I am embracing a ridge-end ornamental gargoyle on the tower of Shanhai Pass.

What story can be handed down for thousands of years? What kind of hero can be remembered forever? It's all illusion.

◁ All pass towers were built in advantageous places for defense, where "one man could hold out against ten thousand."

The Great Wall is listening: to the turbulent rhythm of the rising sun, the graceful melody of the evening glow, the roaring of the wind, the whispering of the rain. It hears them all, and so do I.

Portraits of soldiers of different dynasties.

A round stone watchtower

◁ The watchtowers are generally 10-15 m high; each wall 7-8 m high, the base 6-7 m wide and the top 4-5m wide.

The watchtowers once served as the quarter for soldiers and a storehouse for weapons and grain. This one is a great place for me to take a nap.

In the Ming Dynasty, about one million soldiers were deployed along the Great Wall. When the enemy was sighted, they signaled the fact by lighting smoky beacons during the day and by clear fire ones at night.

The mourner is filled with emotions at the sight of the red blood stains....

The magnificent, gigantic Great Wall looks so small in the universe. It has been proved that the claim "the Great Wall can be seen from the outer space" is wrong. What is really gigantic in this world then?

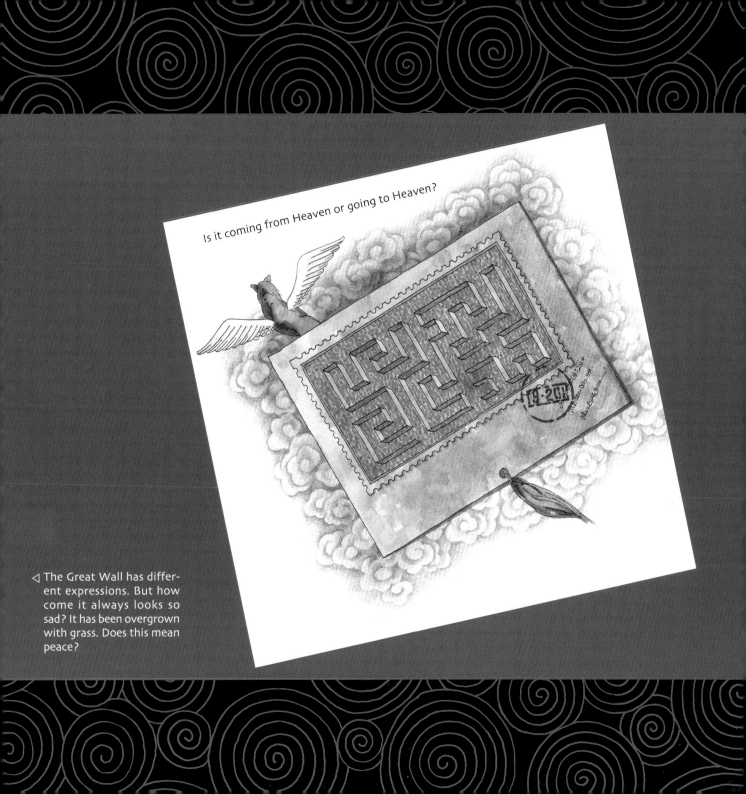

Is it coming from Heaven or going to Heaven?

◁ The Great Wall has different expressions. But how come it always looks so sad? It has been overgrown with grass. Does this mean peace?

The Greater Fangpan Tower near Dunhuang was built during the Han Dynasty over 2,000 years ago.

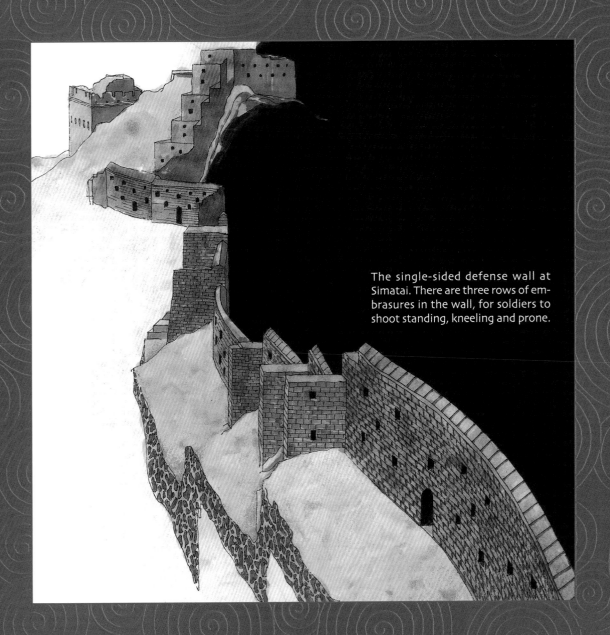

◁ Look at the wild flowers. On the Great Wall, where time and history seem to stand still, the blooming, short-lived flowers look extraordinarily brilliant.

The single-sided defense wall at Simatai. There are three rows of embrasures in the wall, for soldiers to shoot standing, kneeling and prone.

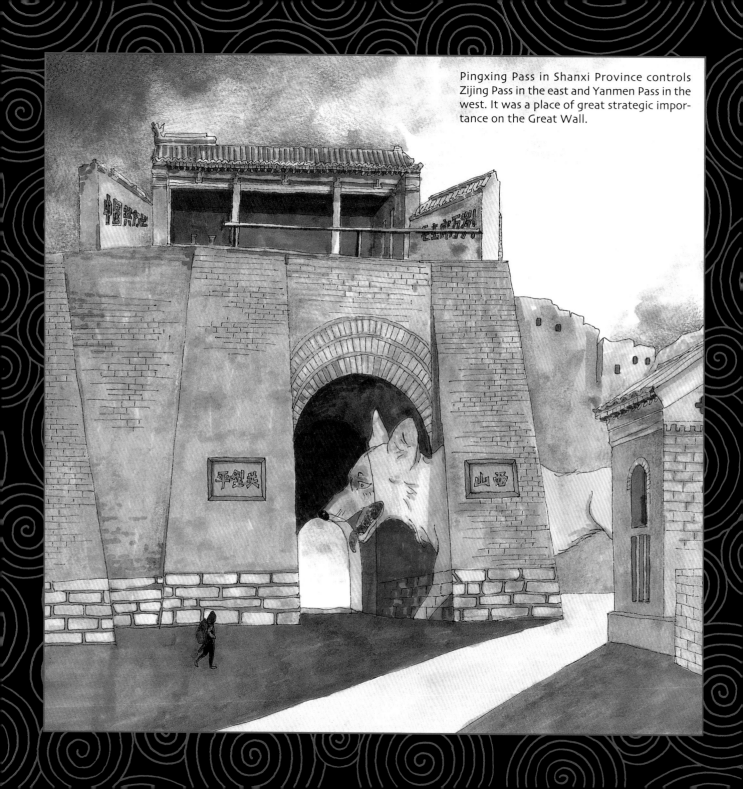

Pingxing Pass in Shanxi Province controls Zijing Pass in the east and Yanmen Pass in the west. It was a place of great strategic importance on the Great Wall.

The Mutianyu section of the Great Wall in Huairou, in the northeastern suburbs of Beijing, is well known. Do you know the Wangquanyu section?

The Great Wall is spectacular because it is very long, extending thousands of kilometers. It is great because it is very old, its origins dating over 2,000 years. It is not simply a wall. It is threaded through the annals of Chinese civilization. It symbolizes the spine of the Chinese nation.

⊲ The leaves have fallen, leaving the bare branches pointing to the sky. Life and death follow each other in an unending circle. Will the Great Wall exist forever?

On both sides of the arch at Yuntai, on Juyong Pass, are relief carvings of the four Heavenly Kings. I don't know who was to save whom, but the images look very impressive.

No more defense walls
will be built. The Great
Wall built in everyone's
heart is always green,
not for defense, but for
communication.

How come there are Qin soldiers on the Great Wall of the State of Qi?

# 走啊走，走长城

因为有狼，
猎人筑起了墙。
围住了羊，却没挡住狼。
历经风雨、
饱经桑沧，
留下长城长又长。

儿时的童谣竟然是那么清晰地留在我的记忆里，每一个字像一块重重的城墙砖，排在心中最孤寂的地方，搬动它不易，几十年过去了，它还在那儿。

长城的造型确确实实与我们民族的图腾"龙"的形象太像了，长长的、弯弯的、时隐时现……一条卧在高山大川间见首难见尾的巨龙。

今天我们所说的长城，指中国北方西起甘肃临洮、东至辽宁东部，长达5,000余公里的秦长城；也指将长城沿丝绸之路，从甘肃酒泉，经敦煌，直至新疆罗布泊向西延伸，长达10,000余公里的汉长城；其中还包括修筑了五六百年的明长城。长城，历史之久远、纵横之辽阔，使它成为举世瞩目的人类文化遗产。

走在长城上你会想到什么？如果长城真的是固若金汤，游牧民族一直被长城所阻，那么，中国肯定不会是今天的模样，疆土一定比现在小得多。然而，游牧民族却屡屡越过长城，入主中原，使中华民族成为多民族融合的大家庭；使长城成为中国版图内的一道亮丽的风景线。回顾历史，长城使我们看到了防御者的伟大，同时又看到了进攻者的雄武。围绕长城所进行的战争如同情场上的决斗、兄弟之间的内争，无论从哪个方面回望，长城永远是值得骄傲的创造！

长城如夫，他有两个妻子，一个是农耕民族、另一个是游牧民族；长城如弦，它时而激越如金戈铁马，时而柔曼如梨园乐府。游牧与农业这两张弓在轮番演奏着光荣与梦想、繁荣与衰落、统一与分裂、生与死、爱与恨……

长城是壮美和雄沉的极致，有什么人造景观能与之相比。走在长城上你看到什么？长城蜿蜒越过无数高山峻岭，穿过茫茫草原和浩瀚大漠，连接百座雄关、隘口和成千上万座敌台和烽火烟墩，昔日里不散的狼烟似乎还在升腾。

走在长城上，我看到过嘉峪关的日出、山海关的夕阳、望京楼下的云海、金山岭上皑皑白雪、居庸关上的青松翠柏、慕田峪长城的红叶、八达岭的奇峰险阻、老龙头长城的万顷碧波……风中隐约还飘着孟姜女的哭泣声，不过很难说清楚她是在为自己那死去的夫君流泪，还是为被岁月侵蚀、被人为损坏的长城哭泣；长城伟岸的身躯在渐渐的衰老、一部分一部分地在消亡，难道百年之后留下的长城只是个传说吗？

被长城勾联在一起的贫瘠、荒漠的土地，以及这片土地上绵绵不断向西延伸的长城，让我爱到心痛。我无论如何不能只扮演成一位轻松的旅游者，我的心跳与长城西去的节奏那么吻合，我要去寻找它、接近它、礼拜它、纪念它、保护它。

走啊走，走长城，与我昔日的"对手"结伴同行。

公元前七八世纪楚国构筑的城墙是至今所知修筑"长城"最早的记载。公元前221年秦始皇灭六国后将秦、赵、燕三国北方的长城连接起来，形成了一条西起甘肃临洮，东至辽宁东部的"万里长城"。秦始皇便成了修筑长城的"第一人"了。

是否因为人类生性好斗,才使得御敌的战壕在史前就出现了？还有人说为阻挡洪水而筑的堤坝，是长城的雏形。

汉代玉门关，到底在哪儿，至今尚无定论。但是"羌笛何须怨杨柳，春风不度玉门关"的诗句却家喻户晓。

如果先发明了飞机,还有哪位皇帝会下令修筑长城？然而,在冷兵器时代，长城可是坚不可摧的象征。

"烽火戏诸侯"的故事，我们绝不陌生。今天我们的身边还会发生类似的故事吗？

明代所修的长城从中国北方的东部鸭绿江畔起，翻越燕山，沿太行山、贺兰山，又穿越沙漠、戈壁遥遥向西，一直到中国的西北嘉峪关，全长6,500余公里。这仅占中国历代所建长城的十分之一。

一个孟姜女哭倒长城的故事,能流传上千年,其中的原因现代人又怎么能明白呢？

历代修筑长城时死亡的人数，多得无法统计，关于耗资更是天文数字，仅16世纪中叶，明代著名将领戚继光修筑从山海关至居庸关以东的长城，就花费了白银1100万两（当时的全国年度财政收入才400万两左右）。

敌楼由基层、中室和顶上哨房三部分建筑构成。基层大都是由条石砌筑的高台，没有门窗；中层用砖砌成拱券式，南北东西筑有不尽相同的若干通道。

雪中的长城，如同冰雕玉琢的一般。

"望京楼"是北京地区长城的最高点，海拔 2000 余米。传说是天神用神鞭将石头变成山羊赶上山顶后，又将山羊变成石头，用来建成此楼的。脚下是万丈深渊，一旦坠入，便万劫不复。

"神威大将军"铁炮曾经打败过谁呢？大批清军就是从它眼下进关驰入中原的。明朝倾巨资修筑的坚固长城，为何没能挡住满族入关？

我在长城上既看到防御者的伟大，也看到进犯者的雄武。

因为有狼，猎人筑起了墙，圈住了羊，却没挡住狼，留下长城长又长。

"君独不见长城下，死人骸骨相撑拄。"如果没有那些战争，人类能否走到今天？

长城像长着巨齿的口，它会吃人。

是游牧民族的铁骑飞越长城，扩张、再扩张，才有了中华民族今天的广大版图。此时，一切都安静了。

汉代张骞、班超从这里跨了出去；印度、巴基斯坦、阿富汗、伊朗等南亚、中西亚各国商人从这里走了进来。可见长城阻隔不了国家与国家、民族与民族之间的交往。

中国北方的长城几乎是农耕区与游牧区的分界线。我一直以为长城以内的人是"羊"，长城以外的人是"狼"，在这里羊和狼轮番演奏着光荣与梦想，繁荣与衰落，统一与分裂，生与死，爱与恨……

长城上刻满了历史的年轮，记载着两千多年华夏民族的成长和发展。

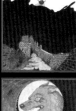

在许多地方构筑的"边墙"，完全是"跑马圈地"性质的行为，既无人驻扎，又不具备防御功能。

百年之后，只留下一个"长城"的传说？不会吧！

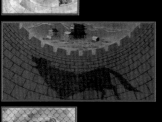

居庸关是守卫北京的西大门，为历代兵家必争之地，其景色有"居庸叠翠"之美称。它与山海关到底谁是"天下第一关"呢？

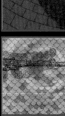

长城东起点，形如探入海中的巨龙之首，十分形象的被称为"老龙头"。

长城的美深深植根于大地，苍凉、凄美且豪迈。真正能读懂长城的，
又有几个人呢？

浓重的秋色，给了多少诗人创作的灵感，在这墙体如"虎皮"一般
的长城上，我又能作出什么样的诗呢：是赞美长城的伟大，还是诅
咒统治者的残暴。

长城的壮观， 是光的赐予，如同天造之物，令人感叹。

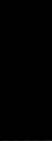

就在这如悬壁一般的长城上，我看到了北国风光、千里冰封、万里雪
飘……

阳光、山岭、风和云，都是长城最忠实的朋友，它们一同存在，一同
静默，一同饱览世间沧桑变化。

无尽的荒漠，长城穿过它，攀越，衔接，圈拢……荒漠还是荒漠，长
城无语地向西、向西，再向西。据不完全统计，仅北京，河北等中国
北方 16 个省、市、区内的长城总长度就已超过 5 万公里。

西汉长城的烽燧、亭障、列城西起大宛贰师城、赤谷城，经龟兹、焉
耆、车师、居延，一直到达黑龙江北岸。构成了一道城堡相连，烽火
相望的防线。

逶迤的长城曾三次与黄河相会，每次相会，长城都被黄河斩断。然
而，所有相会处的景观又是那么壮美：万里长城永不倒，千里黄河水
滔滔。

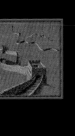

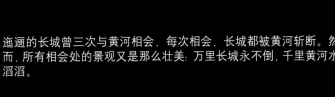

长城防线上共设辽东、蓟、宣府、大同、山西、榆林、宁夏、固原、甘肃九个军事管辖区，统称"九边重镇"。我现在到了榆林。

玉门关以西，汉朝时修筑的烽火台。

长城不是一项孤立的防御工程，与之相配的有兵营、仓库、道路、桥梁、驿站、衙署 、屯田、居民点等等，是军事与民政兼顾的完整的体系。我就曾经是金山岭长城库房楼的防卫。

大漠戈壁中的嘉峪关，南面是终年积雪的祁连山，北面是一片茫茫戈壁滩。嘉峪关是明代长城的西端。我眼前那片朦朦胧胧的关塞是嘉峪关、还是海市蜃楼？

明代长城的宽度可容 5 匹战马并行，10 名士兵列横队并进。

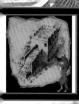

你想看到修筑长城的场面吗？这里面的故事太多、太多了。

看到这齐长城，能联想起什么呢？那段历史早已被时光冲刷得似梦幻般朦胧。

任何坚固的城池，都没有永远不被攻克的记录。这里曾经发生过厮杀、争斗，呐喊声、呻吟声，仿佛还能听到。

山海关，北接燕山山脉，南临渤海之滨。也是华北通往东北三省的咽喉要道。素有"西京锁钥无双地，万里长城第一关"之称，我拥抱的是山海关城楼鸥吻。

什么样的故事能流传千古？又有什么样的英烈能万世留名？一切都像是泡沫。

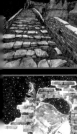

所有的"关城"都设在有利防守的地形之处，正所谓"一夫当关，万夫莫开"。

长城在倾听：朝阳升起时澎湃的节奏，晚霞隐没时优雅的旋律．风的怒吼，雨的倾诉。长城听到了，我也听到了。

历代士兵的写照。

敌楼一般高10-15米；城墙一般高7-8米，底部厚6-7米，墙顶宽约4-5米。

长城上的石砌圆形敌台。

"敌楼"原本就是戍边士兵的住宿地和储存武器、粮食的地方，我在这儿小憩正合适。

明代在长城沿线部署兵力约100万，一旦发现有入侵者，白天燃烟，夜间举火。

此处屡见血殷红，登临凭吊感慨生……

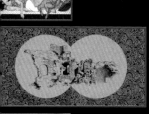

如此雄伟、如此巨大的长城，在宇宙中竟显得那么渺小。曾经令我们骄傲的宇航员"在太空中能见到长城"的说法，也只是误传。那么，世上还有什么是大的呢。

长城是有表情的，但为什么总透着伤感；现在城墙上杂草丛生，这是否意味着和平！

从天上来，还是到天上去！

敦煌附近的大方盘城遗址，它原是两千多年前汉代的一座大方城。

看，野花。如此短暂的生命，在这凝固了时间、凝固了历史的长城上同样怒放，感觉是那样的异常绚丽。

司马台长城的单边战墙，墙上射眼密集，上下分为三排。可供三列士兵以立、跪、卧三种姿势射箭。

山西境内的平型关东控紫荆，西辖雁门，是长城上的重要关隘。

很多人都知道京郊怀柔境内有一个慕田峪长城,还有叫着旺泉峪长城的，你知道吗！

长城之所以壮观，因为它太长，绵延数万里；长城之所以伟大，因为它太老,历经两千多年。它已不只是一堵墙,它是华夏文明史册的书脊，是一个民族的脊梁。

叶子落了，裸露的树枝直指苍天。生生死死,周而复始,才是生命的真谛。那么，长城能永远存在吗？

居庸关云台券洞的两侧,雕有四大天王浮雕像,让谁救度谁,我看不懂，只觉得这雕像挺威武。

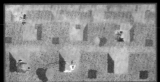

人们不会再筑墙,而建筑在每个人心中的长城是绿色的,不是绿色屏障，而是绿色桥梁。

齐长城上为何有秦的战士？

**图书在版编目（CIP）数据**

谁来陪我走长城／羊子编绘．－北京：外文出版社，2005

（图说北京）

ISBN 7-119-04180-0

Ⅰ．谁… Ⅱ．羊… Ⅲ．长城－简介－图集 Ⅳ．K928.77-64

中国版本图书馆 CIP 数据核字(2005)第 087468 号


编　　绘：羊　子
责 任 编 辑：兰佩瑾
翻　　译：张韶宁
英 文 编 辑：Paul White　郁　苓
设　　计：元　青等
封 面 设 计：兰佩瑾


**谁来陪我走长城**

ⓒ 外文出版社
外文出版社出版
（中国北京百万庄大街 24 号）
邮政编码：100037
外文出版社网页:http://www.flp.com.cn
外文出版社电子邮件地址:info@flp.com.cn
sales@flp.com.cn

深圳市森广源（印刷）有限公司
中国国际图书贸易总公司发行
（中国北京车公庄西路 35 号）
北京邮政信箱第 399 号　邮政编码 100044
2005 年(20 开)第 1 版
2005 年第 1 版第 1 次印刷
（英汉）
ISBN 7-119-04180-0
07800（平）
85-EC-590P